PASSIVE INCOME ASSETS

WEBSITES - HOW TO GENERATE ONLINE INCOME WHILE YOU SLEEP

PASSIVE INCOME SECRETS

COPYRIGHT

DISCLAIMER

TABLE OF CONTENTS

Conclusion INTRODUCTION

Making an income while you sleep seems virtually impossible. With the average American adult working over forty hours a week to create an income, it seems like a fantasy to assume that you can make paychecks while not actively working. However, there is a real, solid way to make money without working long weeks, and many people are using this as their primary and only source of income. We're talking about *passive income*, or money you make without having to go out and earn it. At a traditional job, you work a certain amount of hours and you get paid accordingly, based on your salary or hourly rates. With passive income, the amount of money you can make is limitless, and you don't necessarily have to work longer hours to achieve it.

There are a variety of ways people generate passive income, but the most popular one is online. Since we all use the internet every day, it's a great resource for people wanting to make money but not willing to take out a loan or spend the time required to start their own business. The prospect of earning money for essentially doing nothing is wonderful, but before we start talking about it, there are some things you need to know.

Before we learn how to generate a passive income, let's talk about some of the myths and realities surrounding it. Many people are wary of passive income because they view it as a "get rich quick" scheme that never works and is only about scamming people out of hard earned money. While there are many websites and programs offering false promises about making money online, passive income is absolutely real and absolutely achievable for anybody that wants to work for it. Passive income takes time to generate, and you will more than likely not see a return on your investments right away. That's normal, and to be expected. The whole point of building passive income is so that eventually you can stop working, not quit your job overnight to do something else. It's going to take time, because all good things and all things worth having will take time and effort.

That brings us to the next myth surrounding passive income. Creating a stream of passive revenue, especially with a website or blog, is very attractive to people because, in theory, it allows them to make money without having to actively maintain or work at building their website. This could not be further from the truth. The most important thing to keep in mind when you decide to try and build a passive income source is that it will take time and effort to create something successful. Think of your website as a new business. Small businesses pop up all the time, and they require a lot of work and time to generate success and a profit. Your website is the same way. While your start up costs for a website are definitely lower than they are with a real brick and mortar store, you still have to spend time in order to create something worthwhile. The more successful a business, the less the CEO has to do in order to keep the company successful; the business takes care of itself and the person in charge reaps the benefits. Your website is the same way. The harder you work on it in the beginning, the less work you have to do later on.

Another myth surrounding passive income is that it's money for supplementing a real income. Is this the case? Sometimes. Some people earn a passive income on the side to supplement their full time job or to buy Christmas presents. Other people earn a passive income as a means of replacing their full time job income so they can quit punching a time clock and start doing the things they want to do. And doesn't that sound attractive? To be able to do whatever you want to do whenever you want to do. That can be a reality with passive income, because there are tons of people all over the world that are using the same system you're about to learn about and they're supporting their families, spouses, and children on the salary they create for themselves by doing a little work here and there online.

And why build a website anyway? Aren't there other ways to generate passive income? Yes, there are plenty of ways to make money passively, but a website is a great way for new entrepreneurs to create a consistent stream of income. There's an extremely low start up cost when compared to other start up business ventures, thus you don't need any huge loans and you are not taking a huge risk by creating a website. Many services available for web based businesses are free or very low cost to use, and you can always upgrade as your website becomes successful. People use the Internet for virtually everything, so there is always an audience for your website, whether you know it or not. These people have money, and if you can offer them something of value, they will be more than happy to give it to you.

You want to both inform and sell if your website is going to be successful. Inform your reader of your value to them as an expert of your given field, and then sell them products to turn them into experts too. It's important that you're able to do a variety of things on your website in order to generate income in different ways. The best methods for you will depend on your chosen niche, which we will discuss more in the next chapter.

CHOOSING YOUR NICHE

Now that we're determined to start a website, let's talk about the first step in doing so.

Before you set up hosting or start creating blog content, you must first choose the focus of your website, or your website's *niche*. A niche is a very specific category that will be the main focus of your blog. You want to choose a niche for your blog, because when you focus on a very specific topic, a few things happen. First, you eliminate competition. The more specific your niche is, the less competition there is. There are tons of websites dedicate to photography, but there are significantly fewer websites that deal with the subject of pet photography. Whatever niche you choose, see how specific you can get. The second thing that happens is that your blog automatically grows faster because it receives more views. The audience you will create with a niche website is one that has similar specific interests to you, and someone with the same passion is more likely to spend time and money supporting you and your site. The third thing that happens is that you become the expert in your field. This is the ultimate goal, and the reason choosing a niche early on is more important. You want people to go to you when they have a question or need advice, that is the whole point of your website: to fulfill a reader's needs. When people come to your site, you want to provide something of value to them, and to do so, you need to build trust and respect with your audience. If there are very few people blogging about your niche topic, you automatically become a valuable authority on the topic.

Okay, so creating a niche is important, you understand that. But how, exactly, do you go about doing so? The first step in choosing a niche is to write down at least ten topics you are passionate or knowledgeable about. If you are a mechanic, for example, you can list automotives, and if you are passionate about fishing, that can be another. The important things to remember is that these topics have to be ones that you are both passionate and knowledgeable about, or ones you are at least willing to do research for.

After you have your ten topics written down, cross half of them off. Look at the ones that disinterest you, or the ones you can't think of sticking with through the long haul. You deal with cars every day, do you really want to go home and write blog posts about them after work? Maybe, maybe not. But you love photography, and that is one of the categories you leave uncrossed.

Once those ten have been whittled down to five, you want to break these five down further. For our photography example, let's think about *what kind* of photography you enjoy the most. Sure you like taking iPhone pictures of your dinner or snapping shots at photo booths during weddings, but you are passionate about pet photography and occasionally take professional pictures of pets for friends and family in your free time. This is a great example of narrowing down your topics. Do this with the other four topics you've chosen and then take a look at what you have. What here appeals most to you? It doesn't have to be something you are completely an expert in, that can always follow as you work on your website, but it does have to be something you're passionate about.

If you're having a hard time choosing a niche to write about, don't worry. It's a common problem a lot of people encounter when they go to create a website. You can always write a general website and hope people find it interesting, but how will you market that? How will that show up during a Google search? It probably won't, at least not to the standard you need in order to turn a profit. So you need to get specific. If you're having a hard time, we always suggest going to ecommerce sites like Amazon or eBay. See how they have their categories laid out? They go from general to very specific. Something like Beauty-Cosmetics-Eyes-Mascara-Cruelty Free Mascara, shows the hierarch of topics. As we get further and further down the line, there are less products showing up in the search. When you search for eye makeup, you may get fifty thousand results, but cruelty free mascara may turn up only twelve. Keep this in mind when you're creating your niche, that if there's only 12 sites to choose from versus fifty thousands, that's a lot more traffic per website.

You've chosen a topic you are passionate about, but don't throw that list away just yet. Before you commit to your topic, you need to make sure it will be profitable. This is the more practical side to creating a passive income, and not always the most fun. You want to create something you're passionate about, but if there's nobody to see it then you won't make any money from it, and while "passion projects" are great, you will have plenty of time for them when you are able to make money without constantly working for it. For now, do some research on your topic.

The Google Adwords Keywords tool is a great way to check and see if people are searching for your niche topics. Once you have a niche you want to write about, go to the Google Adwords Keyword Tool and type in a few words or phrases pertaining to your niche. These are called keywords, and we will talk about them more in depth later on. Do the same with your other topics, and see what results are the most popular. Taking this research into consideration, you can choose your niche and get ready to start setting up your blog.

CREATING YOUR WEBSITE

So you've chosen your niche and are ready to start setting up your website. This part can be a little challenging, but also very rewarding once you are finished. The website you create is a direct representation of your business, and should definitely be planned and thought out before you begin. To create your website, you will need a Paypal account, which will be your method of paying and receiving payment through your website, a domain name, a hosting plan that will ensure your domain can be live on the web (often hosting and domain names come together), and Wordpress, a user interface system.

To start, you will want to choose and register your domain name. While many websites, like Wordpress, offer free hosting, meaning they give you a website and a website name for free, you do not usually want to use that and opt for a .com or .net domain address instead. You want to do this for a few reasons. Your website name will be easier to read and remember if it is not attached to another website (bestpetphotos.wordpress.com is a lot more to remember than bestpetphotos.com, right?), and your readers can communicate the site to other people with ease. It's also important to choose a domain name over a free sub domain because when you purchase a domain and hosting yourself, you set the rules and regulations for how your site is run. By hosting your website on another site, you are at the mercy of that websites Terms Of Service, and they can terminate your business at any time. It's almost like living in a house you can get kicked out whenever the owner decides they've had enough of you, and it's not a good idea if you want your business to thrive. A .com domain is also more professional, so if you ever plan on putting your website on business cards or your social media platforms, it will appear more polished and clean. It also fits nicely on headers and logos, which is something to consider later on down the line as your business grows and thrives.

Don't forget that when choosing a domain name itself, it is best to keep it short and simple. Nobody can remember a big long URL, and you certainly don't want to confuse somebody looking for your website by having a difficult to remember URL. Keep your website URL short, abbreviating when you can so it will still make sense and be easy to read. It's best if you keep it in line with the name of your website. For example, The Best Pet Photos You'll Ever See website can read thebestpetphotosyoulleversee.com, or you can abbreviate it to something like bestpetphotos.com which is much more professional and legible.

If you're looking for a few good websites that offer domain names and hosting plans, take a look at HostGator, iPage, or 1and1.com. These are websites that are highly recommended within the website and blogging community, and they all offer different options and price points to create the experience you need and want for your site. It's true that these plans will cost money, but keep in mind that this start up cost is minimal when you consider the amount of money you can, and will, make with enough hard work and dedication. It's always a good idea to shop around and consider what domain names and hosting plans have to offer in terms of security, email addresses, and extra services they can add to your account to enhance your experience. Every website and every goal is different, so you want to take your time looking an make sure you are going to pay for the plan that is right for you.

Once you've chosen and purchased a website, you have to set it up so people can see and use it. To set up a website, many professionals use interface tools like Wordpress. Wordpress is very popular because it allows you to manage your content easily, and is customizable to fit the needs of your website. Wordpress powers a great deal of websites, and many of the most successful online entrepreneurs swear by it as a tool for success. Download the Wordpress interface and install it on your website. This is where it gets a little tricky, as installation will vary based on what web host you plan on using. Bluehost is a great hosting website that was not previously mentioned, and it's a very good resource for absolute beginners as it offers one click Wordpress set up. Once your Wordpress is set up, you can begin designing your website. Keep in mind that, initially, you may want to stick with a generic Wordpress template while you build the bare bones of your website. Wordpress is a very customizable site, and it may be something unfamiliar to you, and it may be easier to create the look you want when you've finished creating the structure for your website.

The best part about the structure of your website is that it is largely the same no matter what you are selling or what your niche is. If you look at the most successful passive income blogs, you'll see that they are all largely set up the same way, and they do so because it makes everything easy and logical for the reader to see. With your website, you want to cater to the reader with how and where your content is arranged. You don't have to look at it all the time, your reader does. Because of this, here is a simple set of pages your site should have. Each page should link to all other pages through a menu bar, preferably at the top or right side of the page for easy access.

A successful passive income generating website does not have to have a huge elaborate set up. There are a few main pages you should have, and the simpler these pages are, the better. Here is a quick list of the pages your website absolutely has to have. You can add more content if you need to, but this is an effective and easy way to keep everything organized for your reader.

You want a landing page (also referred to as a home page), to greet your reader and give them a quick rundown of what your website is and what it does. It greets your reader to your website, allows them to feel welcome and to learn a little more about what your site is and what you're doing with it. Keep in mind that the landing page doesn't need to be elaborate or super detailed, just simple and interesting enough to encourage your reader to keep looking around at your website.

Then, you want to have an "about me" section that will act as a virtual resume of sorts. This is where you will tell your readers about your qualifications, why they should listen to you, and what you're doing with your website. Remember that while your goal is to make a passive income, you don't need to outright state that all you want from your website is money. Instead, talk about the goals you have for your website outside of monetary value. What do you hope your readers gain from you and what you have to say? What makes you qualified to talk about your niche topic? The About Me page is a virtual interaction with each and every reader, so make sure to take it seriously and spend time writing it.

Next, you want to include a blog section. Your blog can be the entirety of your website if you wish, but you can also do a separate section for your blog to keep it more organized. A blog is very important to generating passive income as it is a way to keep readers coming back to your website time and time again. Remember, one of the biggest myths of passive income is that you create a website, don't do anything with it, and then suddenly it starts making you tons of money. Your blog should be updated regularly, with at least one new post per week. This way, readers can count on interesting, dynamic content. Your content should be SEO optimized with keywords to drive viewers to your website. We'll get more into how to produce blog posts that generate revenue in the next chapter, but for now just keep in mind that it is an important part of your website.

Next, you want to have a separate page where you sell any extra products like eBooks, digital files, templates, whatever is relevant to your website and niche. Selling extra content is another great way to monetize your blog because it allows your readers to buy directly from you without you having to sell them anything. Someone read your blog on pet photography and wanted more advice on getting a business started. They saw you sell an ebook of tips and tricks to creating a freelance photography business, and purchased the ebook for $20, which went directly into your Paypal account. They then get the download link directly in their email, and you just made $20 without any interaction with that person whatsoever. You can rely on ad revenue to boost your passive income, but keep in mind that creating digital content your readers can purchase will result in higher and more sustained passive income over time. The links and information to download these products should be on its own separate page. You don't want to constantly advertise your eBook, as wonderful and life changing as it is, on every page of your blog. That can put your readers off and make them feel uncomfortable. By keeping all purchasable products on a separate page, you'll be able to discreetly ask for the sale in other ways.

The final page you need to have is a contact page listing all of the ways your readers and fans can communicate with you. List any social media links you may have, email, and even a phone number, if you wish. You can create a simple contact form and embed it into the contact page to make things even easier, but the entire process is up to you. It's good to give your readers as many ways as possible to contact you; you never know what kind of business opportunities can present themselves if you prepare for them. It's also a great way to interact with people and build your business up even further. *Something as simple as replying to an email from a reader can make all the difference in building your audience.* Keep in mind that it is a good idea to set up separate email and social media accounts for you website so you can keep everything streamlined and professional.

Now that you have your website set up, it's time to get creative. Here is where you may have to do some research and learn a little web or graphic design if you don't already have the knowledge. Your layout should have good contrast for people with poor eyesight, and should take into consideration your readership. If you have a bridal blog, you don't want to create a layout that is black and pink, but soft and pastel, the types of colors people associate with brides and weddings. If you're not familiar with web or graphic design, you can always hire an independent contractor to work on your website for you. Keep in mind that this will cost money, and freelancer's rates will vary based on project complexity, experience, and turnaround time. If you have the funds for it, investing in professional design is a very good idea to help your website become the best it can be and make you the most money possible.

If you don't want to hire a professional, there are plenty of websites that will offer coding and design tutorials to help you master the basics. Lynda.com is a great website with lots of tutorials and help for people wanting to create graphics, and Wordpress.com has a wealth of tutorials for customizing your Wordpress interface. If you are more of a visual learner, you can always search on YouTube for a certain tutorial or explanation, and it often comes with verbal cues and a step by step tutorial on how do a specific task. This may take some time, especially if you're a beginner, but the key to making your website look good and navigate beautifully is to be patient and mindful of what your website will look like in the end.

Keep in mind that a website must also function in addition to looking nice. It is a good idea to get friends and family members of all ages to sit down and try and navigate your website. Have them talk you through what they're doing and how they're feeling. If they start to feel confused or frustrated trying to get to a certain page, make a note of that and make the proper adjustments. If they feel the ads are distracting, consider a different advertising strategy. The talk through method is a popular strategy among web designers to test the usability of their websites. You should perform these tests every so often with some different people to make sure your site is not becoming outdated.

MONETIZING YOUR WEBSITE

Now that you've created your niche, made your website and started adding content, you're probably going to want to set your website up so you can make some money. Monetizing your website can be done in many, many different ways, and it's up to you what way best fits your website and what you want your website to accomplish. To collect the profits you will be making through these marketing strategies, we strongly suggest setting up a Paypal account because it is safe, secure, and can hook up to your bank account if you choose to set it up to do so. So you can be fully informed, here is a brief list of some of the most popular ways to monetize your blog and what they can accomplish. A good monetizing strategy combines a variety of these strategies to produce the best results.

For websites that generate a lot of traffic, Pay Per Click advertising is a great way to monetize a website. Pay Per Click is exactly what it sounds like: a webmaster (that's you) puts advertisements on his or her website that are generated and controlled through a third party website, like Google Adsense. These advertisements are relevant to the content of your website, so keep that in mind when choosing advertising strategies. Each time a visitor clicks on the advertisement, the advertiser keeps track, tallies up your total, and pays you accordingly each month. Your overall success with Pay Per Click advertising will depend on how much traffic your website generates. Websites with higher traffic tend to have more success here, because more people are click on their websites and are more likely to click the links. However, it is the most common type of advertising, so that speaks to the payouts and reliability of the program. As mentioned before, Google Adsense is probably the most popular choice when it comes to Pay Per Click, but there are other advertisers you can look in to, like Clicksor. Keep in mind that a bigger, more well known company like Google will pay higher, because advertisers spend more money to be represented by them.

Another program very similar to Pay Per Click is the Cost Per Mile method of online advertising. One main difference in Cost Per Mile versus Pay Per Click is that the Cost Per Mile method pays just based on how many impressions, or views, your website gets each month. Advertisements are still displayed on your website, their location and topic dictate how much you get paid during each pay cycle, but they just measure traffic, not actual clicks. This is another very popular method, because as long as you have the traffic, you stand to make a good amount of money here. Cost Per Mile is great for people with smaller or growing websites, or websites that are primarily blog based, as those websites have more repeat viewers so you can expect your impressions to grow and your paychecks to be consistent.

While Cost Per Mile and Pay Per Click advertising can take the form of either graphic or text based advertisements, there are a few purely text based advertising strategies you need to know about. Text link ads are a very subtle way to monetize your website, and are good for using during product reviews or text heavy posts. How it works is that during a review or post about a specific product, service, or idea, you link your reader back to another website through a simple text link. That reader, moved by your words, then makes a purchase and you get a commission as a result. This is great for review-heavy websites as it doesn't require a bunch of bulky ads to function. Another text based advertising system is the in-text ads based system. Similar to a text link, this system displays a small, pop up type window inviting the reader to check out the website and make a purchase when the reader hovers the mouse on top. If your reader clicks the pop up, you get paid. This is a little more obvious, so you may want to use the text ads in moderation, but they can be very good on long winded blog posts or text heavy websites as a way to provide a visual interest in an otherwise text only environment.

If you're unsure if any of the above systems are right for you, you can always try a widget based advertising system. Widgets are nice because they combine all four of the above methods of advertising so you constantly have something different on your website. You can also sell advertising space if your blog is popular enough, and that can be a very lucrative venture in its own right. Basically, you and your advertiser get together and decide on a price that they will pay you for you to run their advertisement on your website for a certain length of time. This cuts out the secondary party, and you receive nothing but profit. It also gives you the benefit to charge what you want and what you think your website space is worth, which is another great way to generate passive income. If the idea of ads or advertising in general doesn't make you too happy, keep in mind that you can selectively and discreetly place ads on your high traffic pages to allow your readers to view your content without feeling bombarded or uncomfortable. It's all about moderation, but there are still other ways you can monetize your website.

One of the best and most lucrative ways to monetize your website is through affiliate marketing. Affiliate marketing is something you may be familiar with, and it really is so complex that it warrants its own book, but we'll discuss it briefly here. Basically, affiliate marketing happens when you agree to promote a product or service for a company. You promote it on your blog or website, and link your readers back to the website where they can purchase or sign up for whatever it is you're promoting. When they do that, you get a commission, and often have the opportunity to continue to work with them to promote other products if you are successful. Some companies will give you a link to embed into your content, and others will give you a discount code for your readers that will give them a small discount, and track the sales they receive through you. When you're thinking about what products or services you want to become an affiliate for, try to keep it in line with your website's niche. If your site is about pet photography, like we discussed earlier, you can become an affiliate for websites that sell dog treats, photo retouching software, or even camera equipment. The possibilities are really endless, and the commission payouts are always varied based on what you promote and how much you sell.

If you aren't sure what affiliate products you want to put on your site, you can join an affiliate network and browse their available selection of advertisements. This makes things a little easier, especially in the beginning. You have a middle man that compiles a list of all affiliates that want you to market their products, and essentially, you get to pick what you want to promote. Affiliate networks themselves do take a profit on this service, so you will make more money overall if you just go through other channels to find your affiliates, but if you're new to affiliate marketing and want a little guidance, a network is a good place to go. Again, affiliate marketing is a rather complex subject that requires its own book, but over time you will understand more about how it works to make you money in your niche. Remember that you do not want to over promote products and get a reputation as someone just looking to make money, be honest and open with your readers about your affiliate links and the fact that you make a commission off of their purchase. As long as you are only recommending products that you love, use, and see value in, people will understand and appreciate you recommendation.

One of the best and most lucrative ways to make money off of your website is to create your own digital content and sell it. eBooks, digital courses, downloadable graphic files, audiobooks, the list is literally endless, and the best part about it is that you get to choose your pricing. How it works is that you create a piece of content that you market on your website to your reader. If you're still managing the pet photography website, for example, maybe you've written a book about your best tips and tricks for starting a pet photography business, and you want to sell it on your website. All you do is set the purchase function up on your website and direct your readers to it where they can purchase. After they purchase, they are sent a download link to the file in their email, and the money is sent to your Paypal account. This happens over and over again, until you are generating real, consistent money each and every day. When writing ebooks, they don't have to be elaborate or sophisticated in their formatting. In fact, the easiest way to create an eBook quickly is to take the important points from all of your best blog posts, elaborate on them, and put them into an eBook template. If you don't have an eBook template, there are plenty of free ones available for download online, or you can format the book yourself, if you're alright with spending a little time. You can sell your eBook on Amazon or through an eBook publishing service. Amazon is usually recommended, as it allows the reader to open the eBook on their tablet or phone with greater ease.

Aside from eBooks, you can make and sell almost anything passively. Digital files, such as vector or .psd files for graphic designers are great because you can charge a fee per download. The possibilities for graphics are endless and it's a fun way to use your imagination in your spare time. If you're good at sewing or crafts, you can create digital files of your favorite patterns and distribute them through your website for a small fee.

If you're really good at something and want to teach someone else how to do it, you should consider selling tutorials or guides through your website. These are great if you're an expert at DIY or home repair, as those are super popular niches with people always wanting some help or new ideas. Again, formatting a tutorial or guide is always optional, but it's a great way to showcase your talents. You can even create audio guides or podcasts, as well as video tutorials that your readers can download. This is a great way to appeal to people that are more audio based learners and will let your audience extend even further.

Something separate from a website or blog is YouTube. YouTube operates largely on Google AdSense, so you're getting a Pay Per Click advertising plan. Here, you just upload a video, make sure to share it on your social media, and when people view your website and see or click your ads, you make money. As your popularity grows, you can become a Youtube Partner, where they will actually pay you according to how many views your video gets. There are many YouTube users that have been able to make a full time living off of making videos for their given niche, but the nice part about this is that you can always do this in addition to your actual website. By cross linking, or referencing the two sites back and forth, you can increase your viewer traffic and conversion rates. Think about your niche and what kind of videos you can make that would be relevant and interesting. For example, your readers on your pet photography website may like to see behind the scenes footage from photo shoots, or hear more about your favorite places to shoot locally. These types of things always look best in video format, so it's a good idea to look into creating different types of media to support your website.

Selling something YOU create is always one of the best options because it allows you to set the price, and you to reap all of the profits. Advertising is a great way to generate revenue in the meantime as it is always consistently on your blog, but things like actual content are an awesome way to reach out to more people and generate more income. When creating content, use your imagination. You can sell virtually anything, as long as it's something you made and you have full copyrights over it. It's great because there's no back stock to keep, and you don't ever have to be present for the sale to take place. Use your imagination and figure out what people want and how you can help them solve their problems, and you won't believe the results.

CREATING CONTENT THAT SELLS

The content of your website is where the magic really happens. When you create dynamic, engaging content, you build your viewership and grow your website's popularity. While advertisements and marketing are great ways to make money with your website, you won't see as much of a result if the content your website has to offer is poorly crafted. Here are a few types of content you can offer on your website, and some advice on creating them so they will make you money.

Blog posts are the bread and butter of any passive income generating website. They are what drives traffic to the blog, and what keeps the reader coming back time after time. Blogs are dynamic, meaning they are always changing, so someone interested in your niche topic will keep coming back to see the new content you provide. For this reason, there are a few things you need to keep in mind when creating the blog section of your website.

Create a posting schedule. This is a no brainer. Blog posts should be at least once a week, and should be interesting and varied. If you plan on being out of town or away from your website, it's not a bad idea to write a few blog posts in advance and schedule them to be posted in your absence. That way you are still generating new traffic to your website.

When writing blog articles, you will use a similar technique you used when choosing your niche. Blog posts need to be focused and specific for a few reasons. A blog post that is specific generates more traffic than a general blog post, because it ranks higher in search ratings. A specific blog post also allows you to go into more depth than a general topic would allow, which in turn creates trust with your readers. Because you are able to create targeted, focused articles, your content becomes valuable and trustworthy, which in turn creates a higher readership.

To create a blog post that will sell, you will employ the same technique you used to create your niche. For our example, we're going to say we run a pet photography blog. To create a list of content ideas, we'll break this down into four categories. Our categories are product reviews (remember how important affiliate marketing is), tips and tricks, photo shoot ideas, and business advice. Because we were able to break our niche into even smaller content ideas, we can take the content ideas and make those even more specific. For reviews, for example, we can review camera equipment, photo retouching software, pet treats and toys, and even photo shoot locations. Now that we have even more specific content ideas, we can create blog posts that are specific and focused to one idea, so our readers will walk away with a more thorough knowledge of the subject, hopefully have found the answer to a question, or be given some good ideas to help in a situation relevant to them.

When it comes to formatting your blog post, there are some things you need to do to make sure your content is profitable for you. First, you need to know about SEO and keyword density. SEO, or Search Engine Optimization, is a way of formatting content so it appears higher in search rankings. This is an internet marketing strategy that is touted as making your website more popular along with keyword density, or how often a specific word or set of words appears in your text so search engines can find it based on those keywords. SEO and keyword density is also something complex that warrants its own book so you can truly understand it, but the simple thing to do is to remember that each article you write should have a certain set of keywords listed so search engines can find it and understand what's going on. If you're interested in the history of SEO and how it works on a scientific level, Moz.com has some great lectures for you.

Another important aspect of formatting your content is in how you present your information to the readers. Remember writing essays in school? You had an introduction that introduced your concept and main idea, paragraphs that explained each point individually, and a conclusion that wrapped your paper up and gave your reader a sense of closure. Your blog posts are no different. Tell your reader what you're going to tell them, tell them, then tell them again. It's just like your essays in school, but more fun and with less in text citations. Many bloggers will make "listicles" or articles that are in list format for easier reading. If you are targeting younger people or millenials, this is a great way to present a lot of content in an easy to read format to make things less tedious in a large blog post. If your blog post is not as long, you can always use standard formatting, but you always want to add an introduction and conclusion so your reader can understand the piece.

We joke about in text citations, but it is so important to avoid plagiarism and copyright infringement. Plagiarism occurs when you steal text from a source that isn't yours, and it happens more often than you think. While a lot of plagiarism is not intentional, you can still get in trouble if it happens, intentional or not. You can use a website like Copyscape to check your articles for authenticity before you post, and always cite your sources. If you found a quote or statistic from a website, just create a simple text link back to the author to credit them for their work. This is not hard to do and can save you a good amount of trouble in the long run.

Another thing to discuss is image use and copyright laws. You can't just take any old image you find online, put it on your blog and be ready to go. Especially with artwork or photographs, even if the picture is online, the source maintains all copyright materials unless otherwise stated. Royalty Free images are free to use with no link back necessary. Under Creative Commons Licensing, you can use an image for any purpose, provided you do not alter or change it in any way. If an image is licensed under Creative Commons, you will have an indicator telling you so on large photo sharing sites like Flickr and DeviantArt. Other sites like iStockPhoto sell royalty free stock photography that you can use for your intended purpose. It is always recommended that if you're going to use an image on your website, it should either be your own or purchased from a professional website. Keep in mind that if there is an image in someone's private gallery that you want to use, you can always contact that person and offer to pay a fee for use. This is something you will want to work out with that person at the time, and it's always advised that you save and print the interaction between the two of you just in case.

MANAGING YOUR WEBSITE

Now that you've created your blog, started producing your content and are starting to see an income come in, what do you do now? Now, you have to manage and build your website. Truly, one of the hardest part is not getting your business started but growing it into something successful. To create a successful business, you need to do a few things to ensure that your site grows and stays profitable.

Consider an advertising campaign. To advertise your website, it's a good idea to take out advertising space on other blogs in your niche. Once you become popular enough, this may not be necessary, but if another blog in a niche similar to yours is selling advertising space, it's a good idea to contact that person and try and work out a deal.

Another tip for maintaining your website is to create a content posting schedule and stick to it. It is very important that you regularly update the content that is on your website. Whether that means adding a new ebook or electronic course every six months or adding a new blog post every Thursday, you need to physically write down what you need to update and when. This is important because you can't just leave your blog static and expect it to continue to work for you. If you do this, it may make some money for you for a little while, but eventually your readers will assume your site is dead and that there will never be new content. And why bother going back to a site that will never get updated?

You also need to create social media accounts that will link back to your website as a part of managing the growth of your website. Sites like Facebook and Twitter are completely free, and they are great for businesses to communicate with visitors with ease. Remember that a personal Facebook or Twitter profile is great, but it's best to communicate more professionally with potential readers. These profiles also help to get you chatting with people in your niche and other power players in the passive income industry for when you need advice or some inspiration.

The biggest part of managing your website is that you need to be present on your website each day. Type in the URL and go click around as a user. What do you see? Does it seem easy to navigate or do you find yourself struggling to get to the contact section. Does the landing page make sense? What about your layout? If you built the layout yourself, it's always a good idea to get a professional design firm or freelancer to create and install a custom Wordpress theme for you every once in a while. Now that you have the income to do so, giving your site a facelift is an important way to keep it relevant and looking nice.

You also want to update and remove old content. If standards and practices for pet photography have changed since you wrote your first eBook, take it down and revise and repost it. You can always take it down and write something else in its place, whatever would be more profitable.

Managing your website is an essential part of making money online, and as your site grows and develops, you will have to do it less and less. But just like producing content and setting things up, you have to give it a little bit of time before you are able to take it easy the way you want.

YOUR WEBSITE AS A BUSINESS

Now, we need to touch on a few important topics concerning your website and your business. Keep in mind that your website is your business, and you should treat it with the same livelihood and respect you would if you were starting a brand new company from the ground up. To grow your business and be successful, there are a few things you need to do once your website is created to keep everything moving in the right direction.

Advertising is key to growing your website. It's not enough that you have ads placed on your website, you have to drive traffic to the site itself to keep generating revenue. Think about an advertising and marketing strategy you can use to increase traffic flow to your website. The easiest thing to do in the beginning is to advertise on social media. Post a link to your blog on your Facebook, so friends and family can see what you're doing, or tweet a quote from the blog post with a link back to it on your personal Twitter account. Almost everybody online uses some form of social media, so it is imperative that you promote your website online. One of the best parts about social media is that it's almost always completely free to use, so it's a great way to promote what you do without having to factor in an advertising budget.

While we're on the topic of social media, it's a good idea to make a social media presence based on your website. Set up a Facebook and Twitter just for your website, and make sure to link it in your posts so people can contact you if they want to. Creating a social media presence allows you to directly interact with your audience, and it's a great way to gain followers and improve your conversion rates. It's also a great way to interact with people in the same niche field as you, which can always lead to business opportunities later on.

Another thing you want to do to ensure your website is successful is to perform regular site maintenance. Once your site is created, you will want to have users test it to make sure it's easy and user friendly, but you also want to periodically check to make sure it is still aesthetically pleasing. Graphic and web design styles and trends change very often, so you want to make sure your site is sleek and easy to navigate while styles and standards change. Not only do you need to update the look of your website periodically, you may need to expand the site as you add content. Add a separate page for audio files so people do not have to search your site to find them, for example, and your users will come back because your site is easy to navigate.

Not only do you have to update the look of the site itself, but you should also update the content. Redo the blurb on the front of the landing page to reflect any changes or additions to the site. Add blog posts on regularly scheduled intervals, even if it's only once a week or once every ten days. One really well written blog post is worth six poorly done ones, and you'll see the difference in your paychecks.

It's also a good idea to do a monthly inventory of what your website is doing. Most businesses have a staff meeting at least once a month, and even if your business consists of one employee, you still need to evaluate what your website is doing and ways to improve. This should be done on a monthly or biweekly basis, at least. Take a look at your Google Analytics, see what keywords your readers have been searching, and check your earnings from ad revenues, digital content sales, and any other assets you may have on your website. Compare it with the previous month's earnings and ratings, and decide what you can do to improve, and where you want your website to go in the next month. This is also a good time to brainstorm potential blog or eBook topics for the upcoming month. It's not good to release eBooks all the time, but if you have some big projects in mind, it helps to break them down into smaller ones during these meetings so you can create a schedule for yourself. Freelancers and entrepreneurs must be organized and focused to turn a profit, and you are no different where your website is concerned.

When you are evaluating your blog's performance, it also helps to do the same to your competitors. Take a few blogs in your niche (hopefully, they're hard to find). Look at their website, their products, the comments in the comment section of their blog posts. Does what you see compare with what your website is doing? It's not exactly fair to compare a newer website to a more seasoned one, but if you are wanting to achieve passive income success, it's important to scope out your competition, just like real life businesses do. Keep in mind that this is NOT intended to encourage plagiarism, stealing, or any sort of content spinning, it's just a method to help you evaluate your website's growth and success.

Eventually, you may find that your site is doing very well. You're generating a lot of income without having to put in a forty hour work week, and you're really enjoying the experience online entrepreneurship has to offer. It's fun, challenging, and very rewarding. What do you do if you want to start another blog? Surely, two blogs will generate twice the revenue, right? Well, not necessarily. If you want to start another website to create more passive income, keep in mind that this is another time commitment you must undertake to create more success. You will have to start from the bottom up and while you're more seasoned now, you know what works and what doesn't, you'll still have to give it the time and dedication you did when you were first starting out in the online world. However, that is how many passive income specialists make their fortunes. They have several websites on a variety of topics that they maintain and contribute to on a regular basis. The more you can dedicate to your websites, the better, just remember to not stretch yourself too thin as far as time commitments and quality goes. It's better to have one very successful website that generates a solid income than it is to gamble and create two websites that are mediocre at best.

Be sure that if you decide to open a new website, or of your just growing your existing one, that you keep all financial paperwork necessary to file taxes. You have to treat your online business the same way you would a brick and mortar store, so you have to pay taxes on your earnings to the government. Chances are, your earnings aren't taxed when you get paid, so you will owe taxes. If you are new to small business taxes and what that entails, be sure to see an accountant or tax preparation specialist. As your finances grow, think about how much you allot your blog per month in things like hosting and domain fees, service fees for advertising, and other miscellaneous expenses. Creating a budget should be part of your monthly meetings with yourself, but if the task sounds daunting, remember to print and keep copies of every transaction you make regarding your website's expenses.

Treating your website as a business is essential in creating a high quality passive income. Because it will be your livelihood and primary source of income (maybe not initially, but eventually), you want to give it the attention and respect that it deserves.

CONCLUSION

By now, you've been taken step by step through the real process of creating a passive income with a website. You chose your niche, created your website, and used the monetizing and content creation strategies to come up with products and services other people will value and are now ready to begin making money and living the life you want on your terms. Here is where so many people give up because their website does not start generating a substantial income right away. The best advice any passive income earner can ever give to another person wanting success is to not give up.

Don't give up, keep working hard. Some people take longer than others to achieve success, and some people achieve success with relatively little time or struggle. Don't get disheartened or upset if the money doesn't start pouring in right away, the more effort and time you put into creating something meaningful and enduring, the more value and worth your website will have, and the more money you will see in the long run. There's no such thing as a real, long term get rich quick scheme, but through passive income you have the ability to achieve more financial success than you have ever dreamed possible with your current job. Whatever your current financial situation, whatever you have going on that you feel hinders your success, don't let that stand in the way of you achieving the passive income goals you set for yourself. The harder you work, the bigger your success.

Finally, if you enjoyed this book, please take the time to share your thoughts and post a review on Amazon. It'd be greatly appreciated!

Preview Of Passive Income Assets: Building A Simple Passive Income From Real Estate Investing

Click here to check out the rest of Passive Income Assets: Building A Simple Passive Income From Real Estate Investing on Amazon.

REAL PROPERTY CHECKLIST

Once you have a few different properties, in order to make a final decision, take a look at the following two checklists, with each property in mind. Grant each a score on one of the two scales, a positive score on the first list, and a negative score if on the second. Combine totals. The property with the highest score will most likely be the best purchase for you overall!

WHAT TO LOOK FOR

o *Quality Neighborhoods*
   While this may seem difficult to calculate, it falls squarely into that category of "you'll know it when you see it." Quality neighborhoods include low levels of vandalism, vacancies, active communities, children and families enjoying themselves.

o *Stable Occupancy.*
   Checking the real estate values, number of houses listed for sale, and other factors can define this characteristic. Take into account local universities or colleges, as this impacts occupancy seasonally.

o *Moderate average income*
   Census values can help in determining the stability and income levels in the neighborhood. Check on businesses in the community, as often people seek to work near where they live, and the two interact for a better idea of community averages.

o *Property tax to rent ratio*

If a property has a high tax rate that does not mean it is a danger, it just may indicate a community building or in transition. Take into account community growth and increased community projects to enhance the infrastructure.

- o *Schools nearby with good reputations*
  Generally, the local schools reflect the responsibility and involvement of local parents, so a good school often means good neighbors, good renters.

- o *Low to moderate crime, low vandalism, sensible police presence*
  Your own tolerance for risk will be a factor in this characteristic, as each person's interpretation of low crime is different. Safety and security are high values among renters, so be sure the property you are considering keeps your tenants safe and secure.

- o *Accessible and moderate to high income Job availability.*
  Sensible renters are looking for a home near their best opportunities to succeed themselves. Watch local employers for growth possibilities. Have the location pass what I call the 'Dad Test'. If you were going to live there yourself, would your own father approve of the decision?

- o *Stability in work opportunities*
  Even if the choices are less than optimal, if the work opportunities are many and reasonable, renters will still feel secure in their decision to stay. Give your renters reasons to remain in your rental, and your stable passive income will remain just that.

- o *Accessible and useful amenities nearby.*
  Safe and pleasant parks, nearby shopping and entertainment options, quick and easy freeway access are all great points to keep your rental occupied. A fun place to play is a fine place to stay.

- o *Sensible and well-planned future developments*
  Communities need change, and well-coordinated change makes for favorable living conditions. Just because there will be road construction for a while doesn't mean people will move away; so long as the change makes sense.

- o *Steady and predictable real estate transactions*
  Market forces, seasonal adjustments and work changes all impact renters, perhaps more so than home owners. So by researching the community and checking its stability, you give your choice a better chance to remain occupied over time.

- o *Average to slightly high rent rates.*
  Higher demand leads to higher prices. By ensuring that the demand for your location is acceptably high, and that volume of available rental locations is relatively low, you create an environment of stability that will make your passive income keep on rolling in.

- o *Historically low rates of natural disasters.*

A mountainside property in Malibu or a flood-plain site along the Mississippi River is just asking for trouble. One of the static costs you need to consider is insurance, so choosing a location with a lower chance for an Act of God to damage it just makes sense.

○ *Property condition is good to exceptional*
A property with all the great values we have outlined can still be a difficult choice if it is in poor or unlivable conditions. 'Fixer Upper' means you will take longer to regain the expenses you had to put into the property to begin to turn a profit, so be careful with such; they can become a money pit.

WHAT TO AVOID

○ *Unstable neighborhoods*
When a factory closes down, a solid employer moves away, or an economic hardship by natural causes or political strife occurs, renters fret and consider moving away. Sometimes they come back, and sometimes they never do. Buying into a neighborhood with such challenges may seem optimal, because prices are lower, but the danger of an extended vacancy can hinder passive income, and indeed cause a property to become a liability instead of an asset.

○ *Ultra High Income*
Communities wherein the average income is high can be problematic, as generally such resources have hidden issues – Home Owner Associations, etc., that can detract from the potential revenue stream that the property represents. Though it could cause the per-period revenue income to be higher, the risk if the property becomes vacant can become a problem, too.

○ *Low to Ultra-low income*
You get what you pay for, and though it may seem a windfall to purchase a rental in an area where costs have been depressed, the dangers of other characteristics can downgrade what might have been seen as an advantage. This doesn't discount the opportunity; it just means you need to consider all the variables.

○ *High property tax compared to stability of rental*
A major consideration that often is overlooked is the annual property taxes paid on a property. If the margin of passive income is narrow enough, this can be problematic, particularly if tenancy continuity is an issue. Be sure to take this into consideration.

○ *Schools with poor reputations*
Parents want to know their children are safe, that they are receiving an education, and that their legacy can be improved over that of their parents. A poor school can detract from the property's utility as a passive income resource if the parents have to make other arrangements for getting their children to a school they can trust.

○ *High crime, particular vandalism and break-ins, heavy police presence*

The bane of a landlord is criminal acts, particular property crime like vandalism, break-ins and arson. Be sure to check the police blotter in the neighborhoods you are considering, to reduce the adverse effect that having to deal with such can cause. Although police availability is a positive thing, if the presence is constant or nearly so, it can actually detract from the property's viability as a passive income resource.

o *High turnover in workforce, economy in flux, employer variability*
If a community is having challenges keeping industry and job-creating companies in the neighborhood, this can be problematic for keeping tenants in the property. As vacancy of course reduces the passive income, a property rapidly becomes a liability instead of an asset.

o *Inaccessibility of basic necessities or inordinate amount of 'junk businesses''*
Just as shopping and malls are a positive many industrial or strip mall type businesses in close proximity can be an indicator of instability and rapid changeover. Research the businesses near your prospective properties and ensure they are stable, consistent employers, to give the property the best chance possible to maintain stable renters.

o *Runaway development or irresponsible city planning*
Some communities have difficulty drawing business in, and even more difficulty keeping zoning and community building concepts in focus. Watch for inordinate fluctuations on what the community as a whole is doing, because too much building, or runaway design and development can indicate that a community will have issues in the future.

o *Wild or inordinate fluctuation in real estate market – high volume of listings and vacancies.*
Growing communities, and runaway economies are similar in appearance. Observe the community's current real estate market, watching for an inordinate number of vacancies, wildly changing pricing, and other signs of imbalanced operation. A large number of vacancies suggests you may have a difficult time keeping and attracting renters.

o *Low average rent rates*
Lower than average rental rates suggest that the community has sufficient access to rental, and therefore you may have a challenge keeping your place rented. Even if your comfort level might allow a lower rent rate yet, you could be contributing inadvertently to decay in the community as a whole.

o *Natural disaster potential*
If the property sits astride a major fault line, in the center of Tornado Alley, or sits on a flood plain, you probably want to consider a different location. Just saying.

o *Property in disrepair or abandoned condition*
Even the best deal, if it is on a place that is in terrible condition, can be a detriment. Ensure that the cost to repair, when added to the purchase price, still leaves you sufficient room for passive income. Otherwise, you may have just discovered what is affectionately known as 'A Money Pit'.

Click here to check out the rest of Passive Income Assets: Building A Simple Passive Income From Real Estate Investing on Amazon.

If the links do not work, for whatever reason, you can simply search for the pen name of the author or the name of the titles on the Amazon website to find them.

www.ingramcontent.com/pod-product-compliance
Lightning Source LLC
Chambersburg PA
CBHW070801180526
45168CB00004B/1705